THINK REACT LEAD
When Success and Accomplishments Aren't Enough

To Freeman!

Dom Faussette

Dom

Disclaimer and Terms of Use: The Author and Publisher have strived to be as accurate and complete as possible in the creation of this book, notwithstanding the fact that he does not warrant or represent at any time that the contents within are accurate due to the rapidly changing nature of the internet. While all attempts have been made to verify information provided in this publication, the Author and Publisher assumes no responsibility for errors, omissions, or contrary interpretation of the subject matter herein. Any perceived slights of specific persons, peoples, or organizations are unintentional. In practical advice books, like anything else in life, there are no guarantees of income made. Readers are cautioned to rely on their own judgment about their individual circumstances to act accordingly. This book is not intended for use as a source of legal, business, accounting or financial advice. All readers are advised to seek services of competent professionals in legal, business, accounting, and finance field.

Like you, Executive Coach and Speaker Dom Faussette has seen success defined numerous ways over the years. Is it charisma and positive thinking? Pinstripes and red power ties? Is it all about the situation? Is it meant only for the chosen few who rise to the top?

Or, is there a different story?

With over a decade of corporate leadership, Executive coaching, and most importantly, real-world, in-the-trenches business experience, his view is radically different.

We cannot do anything we put our mind to, without first unlearning what the mind has retained. Dom Faussette extracts the unidentified natural leadership ability you currently possess to build upon your platform.

Dom appreciates, and shares with readers, that success is a moment-to-moment choice and not about title, capital gain or possessions. Success is a feeling of opportunity that requires engaged thought, performance-driven action, and influential leadership.

How to connect with Dom Faussette

Company: Think React Lead Inc.

LinkedIn: https://www.linkedin.com/in/domfaussette

Website: www.DomFaussette.com

Phone: 602-481-0650

Foreword

A wise man once told me, "Everything that shines isn't always a diamond." In all of my years of success, in both business and personal, I have learned that a person's external achievements in life will never fill the void of their internal needs. So many today wear their prosperity outwardly, but mask the poverty that is inward. In this amazing book, Dom provides the fundamental skills needed to balance your external wants with your internal needs so that you can have an exceptional, extraordinary and unique fulfilling life.

As Dom's Father and Pastor, I have had the pleasure of knowing his life events which have allowed him to become a remarkable leader. I truly believe that it was these, sometimes extremely difficult, life lessons that have allowed Dom to hone his leadership skills and abilities which qualify him to be the very guide for those who desire that life fulfillment but can't seem to reach it on their own.

I know that this book can change your life, because I have personally referred friends and acquaintances to Dom for his help in guiding their lives. Those invaluable pearls of wisdom that have helped men and women realize the true value in their lives are found within the pages of this book. One of the wisest authors of all time wrote, "Wisdom is the principle thing; therefore, get wisdom: and with all of your getting, get understanding." Proverbs 4:7 (NKJV)

So, I encourage all those, both young and old, who find themselves reading this book, engage in each sentence, paragraph and chapter, so that you can shine and become your life's most precious gem, both inside and out.

Ron Faussette

Pastor/ Father/CEO Longreen Express

This book is written in a unique way to immerse yourself in the content through a conversational writing style as if I am speaking straight to you.

You will also find that you will learn more easily from this book, not only because of the flow of the content, but there is also an integrated Action Guide which allows you to implement your learning!

Let's get started!

Dom

Dom, tell us a little bit about the clients that Think React Lead serves.

The type of client that Think React Lead works with is going to be that individual that is following a journey, whether it be an entrepreneur journey or a corporate path, climbing the proverbial corporate ladder, and somehow, some way, things don't go as planned.

There are so many times that in our younger years, the early twenties, we have life in the grasp of our hand and we know exactly where we're going to go. One day we wake up, we're thirty and realize we're not where we thought we were going to be. The clients we work with are there. Whether they're successful in the career world and then in their personal world things are going awry, or vice versa.

It sounds like there's a balance issue there.

Oh, always. There's always a balance issue, and it's that triangle. It might be their career. If it's not their career, it's their home life. If it's not their career, it's their health, and so many of us have more than one of those areas negatively impacted. That's what we really want to avoid for our clients.

What do you say to someone who wakes up one day and they think, "Wow, this is where I am, and I don't like it."

Let's go back to the "plan." With many of our clients, what we find is that where they've arrived in life, it was never their plan. It's a societal plan. Their teachers or college professors, their parents, maybe their spouse. These people have some of the best intentions, but what ends up happening is that you wake up, and you're like, "I'm not happy. This is not what I want to do."

Then they're stuck. They don't know what they want to do and why? Because from kindergarten all the way through college, you're given a syllabus. You study the material. And how do you know that you've done well? Well, you take a test, and you get an A on that test, and you're good, and you can move on. But in life, there's no syllabus. There are tests! But no test says, "Oh, you have an A, or you have an F." There's nothing that gives you that validation of, "You know what? I've succeeded."

Let's go deeper into that type of client you work with at Think React Lead, where they may or may not have made their plan. What is going to be an indication for them is that those milestones are a little bit fuzzy, and if they could get them to come into better focus?

It starts with understanding if the dream that you're chasing is your own! I think so many times we get confused with, "This is what I want to do," but we don't realize where that want or even where that desire stems from. If we were to sit down and ask ourselves, "Why do I want to do A, B, or C," and once an individual can determine the whys behind what they want to do, it makes things so much easier, and clearer!

When I say clear, I mean understanding that no matter what it is we want to do, there's going to be some work involved. There's going to be something that we're going to have to do to get us to the next level. Once we're able to determine that this dream is ours, it's something that I want to do, we're able to move forward. We're able to put all the uncertainty behind us and then move forward.

Dom, do you agree that if someone is clear, they feel like they're pulled toward that objective, not pushed because human nature is "if you're pushed, you push back". If you are pulled toward something, it's easier, and you're in the flow, and you can be yourself?

Yes, and there's a couple of scenarios that I'll instruct my clients on. One is if it's someone else's dream, it's not going to have the right fit, but if it's your dream, it will feel right. It relates to being able to move forward and maybe feel a little bit more comforting. If you think it's your dream but it drains you of energy, then it's not yours, because truly if it's your dream, naturally it's going to fire you up. It's going to be fulfilling to you because if it's not, it's going to take you completely out of your strength zone.

It is liberating, and not just for the client. I become liberated when I see this happen. To be able to see a person, an adult, chase something their entire life, grasp it, and then realize they're not excited about what it is that they're doing. This is where we come in. We begin a relationship, build strategies and engage the Coaching process. We help them make a complete 180.

When our client starts to focus on what it is they want to do, we talk about clarity. In my experience, one of the most important areas of development takes place in their relationship building. A recent client said, "My life just feels tangible."

Recently I consulted with an individual struggling with a VP promotion. That's why he became my client. Working together, we got him promoted within six months. He'd been trying to become a VP of the company for six years. But that to me wasn't what was most important. He told me in one of our sessions that he didn't know his son was a well-known high-school artist until we began our coaching relationship. That to me is what drove it home.

The hours we put into working with this client was well worth it, just to get him to say, "You know what? There is more to life than just focusing and following a dream that might not be yours. It's what's in front of you that's important. It's being present."

What led you to this field? What was it for you that helped you get started in this business?

It's almost a two-part story. I grew up wanting to help people out. I didn't know that it would be in this capacity. I joined the military fresh out of high school. I then ended up becoming a police officer once I got out of the service, and I thought that was my purpose in life, my path. Just to be a cop, help the old lady across the street, if you will. That never happened. I never "helped people across the street." I realized that I was hurting more people than helping. Becoming a product of my environment. If you could imagine, as a police officer, more often than not when responding, nobody wants you around. You're just there because something's not going right in the world of someone else. When you do that, and you see a lot of the negativity that takes place in this world day in and day out, it changes who you are as a person.

I got to a point where I went from sad to depressed, to just numb, having no compassion for anybody in the world. It got to the point where I was suicidal. "Suicide by suspect." Let me explain what that is. Going to that depression, that anger stage, I really could no longer handle the job, but I wasn't going to kill myself because my family would end up losing the death benefits, so I opted never again to wear my bulletproof vest. Chasing drug dealers and kicking in doors. Putting myself in the line of fire with the hopes of being taken out. It never happened.

There was one day I'll never forget. It was two in the morning, a weekday, so naturally it was quiet. I was in my patrol car, and some lady jumps out in front of my car. She yells, telling me that her husband was trying to kill her. I get out, and I see her husband standing there. He's got a knife in his hand. He's in the middle of the yard, and like I said, it's two in the morning, so it's dark out. I say to myself, "This is my time to go. I'm good." But then I saw three kids standing behind him. I had my weapon drawn, and I said to myself, "I'm not going to let their dad kill me, and then he goes to prison. but in turn, I'm not going to kill him because nothing good's going to come into these children's lives."

I holstered my weapon, and we struggled, but I made the arrest. I didn't get hurt, and I don't know if I saved his life that day, or if he saved MINE! That next morning, I put my two weeks' notice in because I realized that there's more to life!

A couple of mentors and coaches later, I ended up getting into corporate leadership. Four Fortune 500 companies later, I noticed so many successful people wasting their talents, losing their spark, gaining weight, getting divorced, becoming depressed. And these guys, they were younger than forty. Thought to myself, "I was that person. I was depressed, angry, sad, never wanting to move forward in life, wasting my talents."

I've always been a speaker, so I got certified as a speaker. During that time I met an international coach named Christian Simpson. Everything he was saying and talking about is what I wanted to do. My coaching journey.

Consider those two contrasts: the police officer and the person in the yard, and look past that immediate situation to a future-based reality. You saw these kids and worried what would the result be. You saw this opportunity to make a difference even then and there. That impacted you personally, impacted the family, there are huge ripple effects that that come into play! What are some other things that you do to prepare yourself so that you're ready to give and serve your clients?

It's really about a balance in life. I'm not a big fan of the phrase "life-balance," because for me it's "moment-balance." The balance that I have in my office is not the balance that I'm going to need while I'm out to dinner with my wife or delivering a leadership facilitation at the corporate office. For me, it's about bridging the gap between my mind and my heart.

I talked about your whys, and understanding what it is I was put on this earth to do. I firmly believe that I'm not here for myself.

If I were here for myself, one of the bullets would've hit me when I was a cop, and I would be dead and gone. We all have a greater purpose. The fact that I found mine is what allows me to be here now when I'm coaching, and it is listening to my clients. Do I have a perfect life? No, but I strive towards perfection every day.

When you've been in so many dark places, it's very easy to wake up and be in a happy place. It's a choice. I wake up. My eyelids open. My feet touch the floor. I'm on this side of the dirt! I control everything else that happens that day. I don't have a three-to-five-year plan; I have a three-to-five HOUR plan!

I know that if my clients take the time to seek out a coach and it's me that they decide to work with, I have no choice but to be mentally and emotionally clear to operate at my fullest potential, because the words that I hear during our conversations and the responses that I give can change the direction or the course of their day, maybe even their life! I need those changes to be positive.

Can you remember anyone growing up that had an impact in your life?

Yes. Life is about experiences. My mom and dad, very tough, both prior military, then they both became entrepreneurs. But some of the things that stand out are, I remember I got stabbed my sophomore year in high school because I said something to offend a young lady.

Although that was a negative experience, at that moment, in hindsight, I realized how strong words are. There was a time that I got in trouble, and my mom took me to our DARE officer. It was a lesson in integrity and character. I learned character and integrity at a very early age. It's those two words and those two concepts that, even in my darkest times, kept me right, if you will.

While it'd be good to have someone tell us: "You made an impact in my life when you said__," but unfortunately that just doesn't happen. We just have to know that interactions we have with people can and will make a change in their life, and we need to be present, focused, so that it's a positive change.

What's that switch in people that would cause someone to make one decision or the other?

Going back to my mom, we grew up in San Bernardino, California. It wasn't the most pleasant environment, but one thing she used to do is take us to an even more impoverished environment to just look around and feel the environment. Twenty minutes later she'd take us to a new-build where a Realtor would tour the spec. homes and hand out candy. I remember a time we were sitting on the steps inside of this brand-new house.

We couldn't afford it, but she said, "You can decide to live here, or you can decide to stay where you're at. The choice is yours, but you're not going to get anywhere without hard work and dedication and without being focused on things outside of yourself, from a positive standpoint." I remember that. I remember, like, "You know what? Just because I live here doesn't mean I have to stay here."

That's a gift, and that's very rare that she would do that and not rail against the environment she was in at the moment because that could've been easy to do. She took that initiative, and then for you experiencing that, could've easily gone a different direction and seen that contrast and gotten down to where you were at that moment too. But that pulled you in that mindset shift and gave you that drive, right? What a great thing to say. It's going to take some work. Nobody's going to hand you things. Too many times, people in the environment we're in now with instant everything, text and instant message, it's like, "Oh, I want this, give it to me now." How do you use those concepts when you're working with a client to make that clear to them?

By asking the question, "How bad do you want it?" Understanding that, "It took you thirty years to get here. You're not going to get there, wherever there is, in thirty minutes, or thirty days.

Now we can begin the process, but that's a decision that you would have to make." Understand, there are certain changes that must take place in your life. For the past decade, you may have come home from work and set your butt in front of the television and done nothing. You cannot do that any longer.

You must completely change everything you're doing in your life to get the results you don't have. It's about getting the results that you want, but why haven't we gotten them?

Probably because most of us are lazy and we end up feeling sad because we're a product of our observations, but we don't realize it! For example, when you get into your car, the AM/FM frequencies are flowing back and forth. You have the option to listen to talk radio, sports radio, country, classical, hip hop, jazz, but you tune in by deciding on the station that you're going to listen to.

Compare this example to our lives. We all tune into what it is we want out of life. If you don't want anything out of life, then that's the station you're going to tune into, but if you want something, then you're going to tune into things that are greater than your current situation. It takes a habit to replace a habit.

What you said about the radio frequencies is interesting, because it's the realization that if you're sitting in your car driving down the road and the radio is not on, you do not hear those talk radio, sports radio stations, but they're there. It takes just tuning in, turning it on, changing the channel, and there it is.

Exactly! In our lives, that change and that new direction and that new person, it's there. We must tune into it, and I think that that's the thing that people don't realize. A: they don't know what they want. And B: they don't know how to get there.

Thinking about the Executive Leadership Coaching industry, why should they turn to you?

You're talking about the executive, that CEO, that corporate leader. They grew up in a time where having a coach was frowned upon. Fortunately, today is nothing like yesterday. Yesterday indicated that if you have a coach, you are pretty much on your last leg, that you're broken, you are done. For those that were self-aware enough to have one, they kept it to themselves, where nowadays, people are excited about having coaches. 78% of CEOs being coached said it was their idea, and that research was out of an article from Forbes.

Today, CEOs understand the importance of being self-aware. They understand that leadership is influence, nothing more, nothing less. That's a John Maxwell quote. They enjoy having a coach, and the reason why is because often, at that level in life, the people in your circle are just like you. And not only are they just like you, you're usually the go-to guy in that group.

Nobody's going to give you the feedback that you probably need, and because you guys do the same thing, they're not going to give or allow a different insight.

A coach should be able to ask open and explorative questions, and then listen deeply. If they're able to do that, then they're coaching.

Something that I see in the industry today are coaches that don't have coaches themselves. That's sad, because, in my opinion, you're doing your clients a disservice because you're giving them outdated information. I'm a firm believer that one should not be charging more than what they are currently paying for coaching. For instance, if I'm paying $300 a month for coaching, I should not be charging $1,500 a month for coaching.

As with any other area of expert practice, as a Coach I end up around a lot of other coaches via conferences and shared associations. One of the things that I would say irks me is the "person" the coach is, while they're coaching, is not the person they are when they are their authentic self. I could potentially be the only person in the world that thinks that's a violation of integrity, but I don't believe this behavior is advantageous to his/her clients.

At the end of the day, it's not about us as coaches. It's not about whether you're a life coach, health coach, you name it. It's about the lives you're changing!

I may have a client, but my client has a spouse, or my client has children or my client has a mother and father, or a brother and a sister that look up to them. I'm not just changing their lives. As their coach, I'm changing their existence. I am cultivating and encouraging their relationships.

You said something interesting about the people in that corporate environment. You've got the same people around you, and they're experiencing the same things. If you just have your

small circle of "yes-men" people around you, no one's going to
ask you those challenging questions. It's that external person
with that external perspective that's going to take you to that
next level. Have you seen that in your work?

Oh, I see that often. It's the thought process of: "I am because they say I am." We get caught up in this being around people that while they may be our friends, have their issues in their lives, so they're not going to dive in and give you insight for a couple of reasons.

One: they're not that concerned. Two: you as an individual aren't very open as a person, and they recognize that. If you're in a position of authority, nobody's going to give you the real in-depth assessment on what it is you are doing good or bad. Your strengths they'll give you, but your areas of opportunity, they are not going to give you because they're afraid of the backlash.

In the industry of executive and leadership coaching, for
someone to take their business, career, personal life to the next
level... how should they ask questions to a potential coach so
they make sure they're not going to get anything held back?

Be blunt and direct. One thing that allows me to talk to my clients the way that I do is the rapport. I encourage anybody that's looking for a coach to ask as many questions as you want. If you ask any question and your potential coach takes offense to your inquiry, you need to disconnect that call or that relationship.

If one were to imagine a relationship that's entirely focused on the individual; someone listening rather than just hearing. You want a coach who holds you accountable to your dreams and aspirations. I become insatiably curious about who my clients are and who they intend to be. In my opinion, your coach should almost be as committed to your life as you are committed to your own life!

I tell my potential clients to go with their guts. You can ask all the questions in the world, but if there's not that connection, if there's not that heart-to-heart connection, I think you're going to miss out on a massive opportunity. Although coaching is a business, the mistake a lot of people fall into when looking for a coach is that they treat it as a business transaction. In doing that, you leave out the emotion.

One can't change if emotion is not tapped into. That's like trying to jump start a vehicle, and you've got the jumper cables, but you're attaching it to the bumper as opposed to the battery, because the coach doesn't want to "open up their hood."

Dom, what are people afraid of?

Change.

Having trained dogs as a Military Working Dog Handler in the U.S.Air Force, I realized the emotional difference between the unaware human and my K9 wasn't too far off. When they're hurt, they don't want to be "fixed." There's a phrase, "Hurt people, hurt people." Have you ever tried to have a conversation with someone who is hurt? It may not be you that hurt them, but they don't want to change in that moment. They want to enjoy and embrace that feeling of struggle, that feeling of hurt, that feeling of sadness.

People are afraid of change. They don't know what's on the other side of change. It's fear. They've been doing it this way for so long, and they hear the phrases, "What got you here won't get you there."

Most of my clients are doing well before coming to me. "If you're doing well in life and those around you are encouraging your success, why would you need a coach", so they say. Is one doing well because they're running from childhood hurt? Is one doing well because they're trying to mask errors in their life, or mask different vices in their life?

Are they truly happy, or do they just look successful from the outside? It's those individuals that come to the realization that, "You know what? I need help." It's self-aware, and it's understanding that if you don't change the course in which you're headed down, something's going to give.

I've worked at four different large corporations. I've seen a handful of individuals come out on stretchers, by way of heart attacks, and going back to that stress triangle. Whether it's your health, it's your relationship, or it's your career, "Pressure bursts pipes."

You mentioned doing well. What is a trigger point for that person that would make them realize, "While I am doing well, there could be more," or, "This is one area in my life or business or career or relationship that could need some work?"

One question I ask my clients is, "When is the last time you laughed?" The question you ask, it's a big issue, but so many people, in answering that question for themselves, they go way too deep. It's very simple. I'm not talking about smiled ... "When's the last time you laughed? Or, if you are married, when was the last time you and your spouse laughed together? When is the last time you laughed with your children? When is the last time you turned off your phone and just held your wife's hand in silence and just looked at each other?"

There are so many executives and corporate leaders out there that have not had any interaction with their wives or husbands.

It's those questions that I ask my clients because when they first come to me during our consultation. They just assume it's all going to be corporate talk. When I start asking those fact-finding questions, often, there is a lot of silence, some tears, because nobody in their circle is going to ask them this question.

You may have been married for fifteen years, but you haven't had sex with your wife in seven–eight months. You don't know what your kids are up to. You're lost.

Your answer is very powerful because it goes beyond the usual: "What's a trigger point?" That question about laughing says a whole lot. What must be going on in someone's life to allow them to feel free enough to laugh out loud?

Man, everything must be aligned. Everything must be right. Not right to others, not right to your mom, not right to your spouse, not right to your boss, but must be right in your life.

I remember when I first got out of law enforcement and I was dealing with PTSD, one of my coaches asked, "What is that thing that you used to do as a child that put a huge smile on your face?" Without a blink of an eye, I said, "Skateboarding." He was like, "Dude, that's what you've got to do. Go out tonight, get a skateboard, and just go skateboarding. Just a kick push down the street."

It's funny. I ask my clients, "What is it that makes you happy?" Whether it's face-to-face or we're doing a teleconference, they'll usually lean forward on their desk, and they look at the screen or look at me, and they humbly say, "My kids make me happy," or, "My spouse makes me happy." Okay, those are good answers, and then I ask, "What is that thing that made you happy as a kid or a young adult? When is the last time you did something and gave no care in the world?" At this moment, they'll typically sit back, and they'll have this twinkle in their eye, and I see nothing but teeth!

One guy said, "Bro, I was in a band when I was in college, and I remember heading out with some buddies. We jumped into this old car. We barely had enough money to rub together. But we made it across town and out of state to follow this other band that we were going to open for, but we had to be in class on Monday..." It went on and on. I don't say anything. The conversation just goes.

They first give me the response they think I want to hear. It's cool to say that your kids don't make you happy. Kids are kids. We didn't always make our parents happy, and it's okay to say that although you may be comfortable with your spouse, they might not make you happy. What makes you happy? Picking up that guitar? For me, picking up that skateboard! I still skateboard all the time with my son. Or, daring to do something for yourself with no cares in the world.

What's a misconception that someone might have about achieving some of these outcomes we're talking about?

A misconception that I hear is, "Not right now. I'm too busy." It's the comfort zone ... There's a phrase we use in law enforcement or when riding motorcycles: "Comfort kills." The moment you're comfortable, you're no longer being stretched.

You totally let your guard down! Me and my wife race motorcycles, and we know that discomfort is what causes us to grow. A misconception with coaching is that it's this structured and perfect. Not: "I'm going to give you some questions, you're going to fill out some forms. Three sessions later, you're taking a test, and in a month and a half, you're going to be this new person that can take on the world and be somebody so unique that everything goes your way."

If you have a coach that has agreed to anything less than six months, you don't need that coach. There is no way that a person can change ones' level of happiness and fulfillment in their life in less than six months, and less than two sessions a month. It's impossible.

As I think about my first coaching client, I didn't even recognize the dishonesty with his self for the first two-and-a-half months of coaching. It wasn't until we were in our third month, so we were about session number seven, when I asked what was it that made him happy. This was in the beginning stages of my coaching career, which was why I asked that question so far into the process. Although it's a simple question, the answer reveals so much.

I listen for the answer, the change in body language from, "Oh, my kids make me happy, my wife makes me happy," to, "Dude, doing 150 miles an hour on my motorcycle. That's what makes me happy." So many coaches miss that.

What do you say to someone who answers your question, "What makes you happy," who says, "I don't know"?

If they say, "I don't know," my next question is, "When's the last time you were happy?" That type of person that says, "I don't know," will typically say, "I don't remember." It's not that they don't remember—they don't *want* to remember!

I've never seen a person in an ice cream parlor angry. I've never seen a person playing mini-golf angry, unless they lose a bet. I've never seen a person go dirt biking mad. I've never seen a person cliff dive angry. There are so many things we can do or even we have done. It could be as simple as, "I remember when I was seven, I was playing hide-and-seek with my brothers in the neighborhood. That's the last time I was happy because, at the age of eight, my father died."

The reason why they want to say, "I don't remember," is because there was a tragic event that happened shortly after that. It may not be as tragic as somebody's parent dying. It could be something like people that were diagnosed with something, or they lost their job. Go back to the financial crisis of 2007-2008. I saw a lot of happy people out there with all their brand-new Ferraris, their Ducati's, their Lamborghinis, their four or five vacation homes. Then the economy took a turn for the worse. Suicides increased, depression increased. Prescriptions increased, divorces increased.

I saw my father lose three vehicles, and a million-dollar home. It felt like it was overnight, but what I didn't see him lose was his joy. He's big into model railroads, and he told me, "All right, cool. I lost my millions. I lost my Porsche. I lost my Hummer and my million-dollar property, but I still have my trains." He's like, "I didn't grow up with this stuff. I earned it; I lost it. Well, guess what? I'll earn it again," and he's back to where he was.

That's a big takeaway. You're going to be up, you're going to be down... it's what you do in those peaks and valleys that matter. What's a big mistake or a pitfall that they are making that they might not realize that they're making that's keeping them stuck in that comfort zone?

I would say a mistake is not wanting to grow. It's also deeper than that, because how many people out there don't realize that they don't want to grow? Use this common example: If one gets mad because somebody cuts them off in their vehicle during rush hour, they don't realize the implications of this natural selfish reaction. This individual, more often times than not, has some underlined negative and unresolved issues that need to be addressed. The self-aware person might take into consideration the other drivers possible perspective.

You're in your comfort zone, and this is why I say this. A person that's not living life to their fullest potential lets everything get in their way. They complain without a resolve. They feel like they are entitled. That person that cut them off may have just got a phone call from the doctor telling them, "Look, your wife was just diagnosed with... We need you to get here."

Or the principal that called the parent, "Hey, your son just got hurt on the playground." We're so closed-minded and closed off to the fact that somebody could have an emergency and truly didn't see you. That's a simplified example, but that's something that everybody can relate to.

Do you find solace in coming home and popping open a beer because your day was so long and you need something to make you feel better? You're in your comfort zone!

You should not have to lend yourself to alcohol. You should not have to lend yourself to the television to make you feel relaxed. If you can't get relaxed on your own without anything else, then you're living a lie.

If you look at a person that's overweight they will typically download some app. What they're doing is instead of applying anything, their "app-lying" to themselves!

They haven't applied anything in their life, probably for years. If you're still hitting the snooze button, you're in your comfort zone, because something happened the day before that makes you not want to get up. Why does a person not want to get up in the morning? It's because they don't enjoy what the day has planned for them. Let that same person plan a mountain biking trip with the fellows. They're getting up at three o'clock in the morning, and they probably didn't go to bed until midnight because, like any guy, we all wait until the last minute to pack, so we pack that night. We get a couple of hours of sleep, and without an alarm clock, we're up at three or four o'clock in the morning, and at the rendezvous point waiting on our buddies so we can go up north or go out of town to have fun. When your life's not fun, your day's not fun.

What do you say to someone who says, "Executive coach? Isn't that the same thing as a life coach?"

Honestly, I don't even know what a life coach is or does! I feel that it's impossible to coach somebody's life, and this is the reason why I say this. My clients are only with me six to twelve months. In that six to twelve months, there's going to be an area we're going to focus on, and that choice is theirs.

It could be career development; it could be a relationship; it could be whatever they choose. We typically stay in one stream, but there are so many areas in one's life that dictate the nuances or the outcomes in other areas. Unless you're with somebody for years, there are coaches out there that are, with the type of work that I do.

I could only execute on a couple of areas. That's why I was trained as an executive coach. It's about executing! It's almost like a bullet in a gun. If you have a long-range rifle and you shoot, there may be plenty of targets downrange that you could shoot at. But you're going to have to dial your scope and aim at one target because once you pull that trigger and that bullet goes downrange, it doesn't just leave the barrel and hit the target. There are crosswinds. There are many things that change the bullets trajectory. The same thing applies with coaching. There are so many things that can come up in one's life during the coaching relationship that could dictate the outcome.

We must execute on our delivery, and engage the client affording them the opportunity to execute on the results they want/need for themselves.

You've got a mission.

Yes! I kick in the door, survey the environment, affect the arrest, make the changes, and leave.

What's the first skill or task that you are looking to address for the executive when you engage in a commitment to them?

The first thing we talk about are the results of a form and survey previously sent to them. It covers their career, zero to ten. "Where are you in your career? Are you in the thinking stage, react stage, or the lead stage?" What about with your money, health, friends and family, significant other or romance, personal growth, fun and recreation, and physical environment.

All those, they're filled out on a scale of zero to ten. When they fill this out, it lets me know what we need to work on first. I let them tell me, but it shows that the lack of balance in their life.

Most of my clients have never filled out anything like this. It's very elemental, to be honest with you. Its simplicity has caused some to say to themselves, "Wow, why didn't I figure this out on my own?" As they fill this out, the imbalances are quite recognizable.

Our first session, I'm going to use the rifle analogy. All we're doing is "taking the rifle out of the case." We're not loading the magazine. We're just taking the rifle out of the case and inspecting it, and understanding how valuable knowing your life is, and knowing where you want to go. When you see something on paper, a lot of times I don't really have to say much. They'll know what they need to work on. That assessment has amplified and shined a light on the gap between where they are, compared to where they feel they should be.

So many of us go through life, and we don't put any thought into ourselves. Naturally, we put thought into everything and everyone else, and we're so consumed by our calendar, our phone, our text messages, and what our wife's doing, what our kids are doing, and what our employees are doing. Decades go by, and we don't think about ourselves. It's like the airplane example of the flight attendants who talk about putting your oxygen mask on first before helping your kid. Your knee-jerk reaction is, "I want to help my kid first." But the takeaway there is, you've got to help yourself, so you will be there to be able to help them.

Otherwise, you might be passed out and then they don't have the support they need.

The good thing about the style of coaching that I do with my clients is it ends up being fun. It ends up allowing them not to have to think in the same way they would in the office. It allows them to be free. They trust me because I'm not in their circle. All my clients I see outside of my coach-client relationship. A lot of us ride motorcycles!

It's that refreshing feeling of them knowing somebody that doesn't want anything fundamental, because so many people pull from successful people. Successful people are very cognitive about who's talking to them. They're typically closed off, and they have to put on this front of, "I've got it all together because if I don't put up this front, this person's going to call me out." Or, "This person probably wants something from me," and more often than not, that person does. With this coaching relationship, everything I want from them, they want from themselves as well.

You're aligning and coming alongside them while you're motivating them through the process.

Yes. Definitely.

What would you say is the correct mindset that someone should have when looking at starting the process?

My first response is being willing to unlearn. Everything you know to-date is providing you a service in some areas in your life, but in your overall life, it's doing you a disservice. Be willing to unlearn. Be willing to exchange one bad habit for a good habit. Be willing to talk about what hurts you, to acknowledge the fact that you wish you had a better relationship with your father, but you don't. You were so hardened, then he passed away. You never repaired that hurt, and that's what bothers you. Unlearning includes letting go of the hurts and pains caused by others. Forgive and move forward, your overall success depends upon it.

Be willing to be opened up. If you're going to choose that coach, whether it's me or somebody else, trust that coach. Most of my clients haven't truly trusted someone in a long time, and they've been so closed off to that they don't even know what trust feels like!

Because of the executive corporate nature that they are in, they may feel that you can't show vulnerabilities. Is that indicative of that environment?

It's a dog-eat-dog world. I have a friend, Anthony C.; we graduated the police academy together in 2002. During patrol, he was my partner in most instances. During a recent phone conversation, I came to the realization he did not realize how serious my issues were during my time as a Cop. Wow, you masked it so well, he said. "Every time I saw you without your vest, you would just say you forgot it." He went on to say, "You were so happy, so it seemed, and you were always the first one in the door and you did a lot of crazy stuff. I thought that's just who you were. I didn't know that you were trying to die!"

Even with our closest friends, we pull the wool over their eyes so quickly, and it's because we don't trust them. As a cop, in my early twenties, I didn't trust anybody. I grew up with this phrase:

"Believe none of what you hear and half of what you see." That's because my father didn't trust anybody, and his father didn't trust anybody either. My father doesn't say that now, but growing up, that's what I heard.

That was one of my mantras in life, and although people don't say those words exactly, they think this way.

Having that outside perspective with someone, and trusting the process is so critical because we can find some downloadable form online and think, "Okay, I'm going to take this assessment, and I'm good to go!" But that is only scratching the surface as far as what someone could be seeing about you and how you answer this thing and approach that thing can make you accountable to yourself.

You know what? Your Coach should offend you or at a minimum cause discomfort in the beginning of your Coach & Client relationship. Look at it this way, when you go to the gym and you work out a muscle that you haven't worked out in some time, it's going to be sore for a couple of days after that. Well, that's because you're stretching a muscle that has been dormant, and it hasn't been stretched. It hasn't grown.

The same thing happens with someone emotionally. If your coach doesn't address and stretch those areas, they're not doing their job. The client needs to see where they need to grow, and the only way they can see where they need to grow is sometimes with a coach.

It reminds me of the example in nature of how a butterfly comes out of the cocoon, and if you were to see that struggle and help pull that cocoon and silk apart to help them out because they're struggling, it dies. Because something in that struggle makes the blood flow through their wings or activates something, and that's the only reason that they're able to survive then. We think we're helping and enabling, but it then is counterproductive.

Right. It's totally counterproductive. Coaches should be the ones asking the questions. I see so many coaches who provide insight. Understand this: my clients don't need my life experience. What they need are questions. During our coach-client conversations, in a forty-five-minute session, I should be able to ask two, maybe four questions, and let the client answer them.

A good coach is going to ask the right questions. Without asking permission of their client, they should not provide insight, because it's just my personal insight. Who am I to think that, as a coach, I know it better than you? I'm here just to ask you the right questions so you can become self-aware in your answers.

You're facilitating the process. You're moving it along. You're not answering and filling in the blank for them, or else where's the work involved for them?

Right. If I run for you, are you going to lose weight? If I do push-ups for you, are you going to build up your upper body? No. I must show you the proper form.

What are some examples where a client came to you, and they realized they needed a change, and then what were some of the outcomes and results that they found?

One case study that stands out the most is, an individual that had it all: six figure salary, a couple of exotic cars, great kids, supportive husband, on the outside looked like they had it all, but what she wanted to do is promote. She wanted to get promoted and she could not understand why this wasn't happening for her.

Fortunately, I could figure out just by listening to her, and listening to the relationship that she had with the person that is the controller of her destiny at her place of employment. That guy, her boss, did not have the life that my client had. My client has a very exciting life. Her boss was put-off!

In listening to my client, I stated, "Why don't you just ask your boss to be your mentor?" My client said, "I don't need him to be my mentor. I know what I'm doing." I said, "You know what, you do need him to be your mentor. It's not for you, it's for you to position yourself under him, because everybody wants to be needed, especially in those positions."

Once her boss felt that he was needed by my client, the relationship changed. Her boss was providing her information that she already had. My suggestion was, "Shut your mouth and just listen. It's going to be hard. I get it. But you want him on your team, and he's only going to vouch for you if he's telling you what to do."

As crazy as that sounds, it worked, and what she tried to do in six years was accomplished in six months.

It sounds like that relationship of the boss to employee, changed.

Like Maslow's hierarchy of needs teaches you want to feel appreciated, you want recognition, and that person placed himself under the authority of that boss. To me, that sounds way different than the typical life coach. That was a deep, deep strategy.

It was, and it worked. Another guy I coached, and this was simple. He graduated from college, so this is your typical scenario: athlete, graduated college, lands a couple of gigs. He's doing well, but when I met him at a social event, he goes on to tell me about everything he's doing. Immediately, I recognize a certain heightened level of potential in him. I shared that information, and I said, "Dude, you could be doing so much more.

The reason why you're not is because everybody around you is praising you for your minor accomplishments." With an intrigued look, he says, "Tell me more." I said, "Look, you have a double Masters. You've got these worldly experiences that most people don't have, and you could be making much more money than you're currently making."

Long story short, he became my client, and my goal, with his permission, was to help him to understand the benefit of changing careers for maximum earning potential, but I had to ask him, "What's more important? Following your degree path, or tripling your income?" He's exclaimed, "Dude, I'm single, I'm young. Tripling my income!"

In less than four months, with a couple of interview coaching sessions, I have a lady that updates all my clients' resumes, so I had her redo his. Then I began coaching him to tone down his "alpha-male" behavior that he tried to portray. Then got him to realize that leadership is nothing more than influencing others.

You must be able to influence people on a positive level, not an "I'm better than you" level. A couple of interviews later he ended up landing a job. After attaining this new position, he called me and said, "Dude, I never even knew this existed. I never even knew that these people made this kind of money."

He tripled his income.

What I love about executive coaching is that it puts me around an array of people. I'm learning about so many different industries and the needs of various corporations.

I love building relationships with my clients. My previous clients trust me as they have gone through my process. The advantage here is for my current client(s). Through my associations, I'm able to make introductions where both parties benefit. In past instances, they (previous client) hire them (current client) for their organization on the spot.

That's the ultimate recruiting and networking where an executive knows people are being coached by you, and they appreciate the outcomes, so they want to learn more about that person.

Right, and I just introduce them if I can attend in person, over lunch or dinner. If I can't, a quick email introduction. It just works. I'm building my network; I'm bringing people together that would have never met. I never planned on this happening through coaching, but it's just one of those things that it's awesome the way that it works. For me, it's just part of the coaching process.

If someone thinks they may be ready to get out of that rut or take it to the next level, or just, "I'm successful, but it's not enough," what can they expect when initially connecting with you to learn more?

You bring up a valid point. A lot of my coaching styles are not traditional. The reason they're not traditional is that everything I talk about during our coaching sessions, I've implemented in my life. I went from suicide to not wanting to live or exist, and then through working with a coach, found happiness. Then through a mindset change go from $15 an hour to a six-figure salary in less than nine months, just a shift in my mind!

Obviously, after having a good coach and a couple of mentors this was achievable. If I can do that for me, what can I do for my clients?

When they come to me, they should expect the building of a relationship. I don't work with everybody. I'm fortunate, and I've been blessed to have a career that pays well. I coach because it brings joy and excitement to my life. I mean, who wouldn't want to spend their life helping others operate at their fullest potential?

It's my purpose. It's just fun, but I live it at home. It's funny, I come home, and my wife will come in the house from a long day at the office, and she'll say, "Do not coach me. I just need you to be my husband." I then say, "Come on, but I think I have a question that will allow you to dig deep," and she'll strongly suggest, "I don't need that right now. Let's just go for a walk."

My clients come to me, and it's refreshing. I don't say this lightly. Because I choose my clients, they should expect a new friend. I had one guy call me his younger bigger brother. I hear a lot, "Man, you get me." They should expect to be listened to, they should expect to be respected, they should expect a relationship to be built, to be held accountable.

They should expect that I, as their coach, am going to be committed to their life during this coaching process. They should expect teaching, training, sharing, and expect to be freed of the life that they're currently leading. Because they're not "living" life, they're "leading" their life. You're able to enjoy life and as simple as it sounds you're able to laugh.

You want to open a relationship, and when you do that, it opens an opportunity. It opens a mindset. It opens things that someone may never have thought of on their own.

It's about building relationships. I had someone who recently reached out to me, he's like, "Dude, there's a MotoGP race out here, I assist at the track. Now and then I'll race on this track. I've got the tickets," and he sends me all these links and he's like, "Dude, will you come out here? Let me know; I'll introduce you to all these people." He's a buddy. How many of our clients would do that for us? I've gone fishing with some of my clients.

One of my clients has a yacht we'd hang out on and just talk, have a good time! To me, it's a relationship. It's a relationship where there's an understanding that I have a skill-set and I can help you. If you're willing to be open and understand that I'm not going to judge you, I don't run in your circles. I'm just here to help.

Most of my clients have children, and I tell them: "I don't want to just be your coach, I want to be your children's coach."

I'm going to be doing this until the day I die. I've had one client tell me, "Hey, when my daughter gets out of college; I'm sending her to you!"

I'm in it for the relationships that get built from the positive change that takes place through our coaching. When this happens, and friendships develop and they cannot help but introduce me to their connections. This is the way it should be!

7-Step Assessment Workbook

"If you want to be happy, you must let go of what makes you unhappy."

1. Do I own the RIGHTS? If you're living someone else's dream, you'll always depend on factors outside of self to produce results. **Write down the ways you feel that you may be living someone else's dream.**

_____

_____

_____

_____

_____

_____

_____

_____

_____

_____

_____

_____

_____

_____

_____

"If I don't win, I don't eat... I never go hungry!"

2. What EVIDENCE do I have it is mine? When you own your dream, you can physically see it when no one else can. **List the ways that confirm your dream is yours:**

_____

_____

_____

_____

_____

_____

_____

_____

_____

_____

_____

_____

_____

_____

"Don't dream about what you want to do. Do what you dream about."

"Stop cheating yourself out of the life you deserve."

3. Is my dream my TRUTH? You must rely on self to begin working towards your dream. List the steps you must take now to get your dream off the ground:

_____

_____

_____

_____

_____

_____

_____

_____

_____

_____

_____

_____

_____

_____

_____

"Others are allowed to doubt your dream. You are not."

4. Am I MISSION FOCUSED? Once your dream becomes your mission, you begin a strategic approach to your life's work. Strategies, once implemented, will empower you to conquer all road blocks and setbacks before they happen. Write out your MISSION that your dream accomplishes:

_____

_____

_____

_____

_____

_____

_____

_____

_____

_____

_____

_____

_____

_____

_____

"There is a price for success. There's also a cost for not paying that price."

5. Am I willing to pay the PRICE? Taking authentic action towards your dream sets you apart from the masses. Write out the price you are willing to pay in the pursuit of your dream:

_____

_____

_____

_____

_____

_____

_____

_____

_____

_____

_____

_____

_____

_____

_____

_____

_____

"Happiness is when life brings you more laughs than smiles."

> *"Don't give up on the person you are becoming."*

6. Will it VALIDATE my existence? Approving your dream will increase your level of intensity and self-confirmation. Write about how your dream validates your existence:

_____

_____

_____

_____

_____

_____

_____

_____

_____

_____

_____

_____

_____

_____

_____

_____

"*There will come a time when you can rest. Now isn't the time.*"

"Breathe life into your dreams and inhale your results."

7. Who will I INFLUENCE? Your dream is your purpose. To successfully accomplish your dream, it will have to profit more than just self. Write about who you are going to influence and impact positively with your dream:

_____

_____

_____

_____

_____

_____

_____

_____

_____

_____

_____

_____

_____

_____

_____

"Dom Daily"

Here are a few nuggets of knowledge from videos I shoot for my followers every day. If you like the style and would like to receive free daily leadership and motivation, you can get on the invite list at:

www.DomFaussette.com

"3 Steps to Hitting Every Goal in Life"

How many of you have set a resolution or goal and maybe dropped the ball on those goals or resolution? And some of you have not kept the commitment to yourself. You know, part of the reason is not, obviously, your lack of the ability to set goals. It's simply because you don't understand what it is that caused you to not hit your goals in times past or your resolutions in years past, right?

You know, there's a three-step process of making sure that you hit your goals when you set them. The first one is being authentic, right? Authenticity is huge. Being true to self. If you've never done it before, maybe you don't want to set your goals so high. If you have no proof that you've done it before ...

For example, let's just use going to the gym. That's a very

common thing. "I'm going to go to the gym five times a week."
Well, maybe you've never gone to the gym five times a week
before. You don't really know how to work out. Why would you
set that as your goal? Maybe your goal would be to get a trainer
and promise yourself that you'll go one time a week.

Or maybe your goal can be simply, instead of going to the gym
five times a week, you can simplify your goal and say, "I'm going
to do 50 pushups three times a week. Monday, Wednesday, and
Friday, I'm going to do 50 pushups," right? And then two weeks
later, you do the same 50 pushups a day, and you do it five times
a week. And then you go seven times a week, and you kind of
build yourself up there.

So, be authentic. Understand self. Be self-aware and understand
really what your limitations are, not from a limiting belief
system, but what can you do? What proof do you have that you've
done A, B, or C?

The other one would be a vision. You know, I've talked about this
before, having some sort of vision board in your house,
something that you could work toward. And the vision board can

have things on there that are tangible. It could be a car, a house, a person you want to be with or a certain relationship you want to be in. Other visions you can put on there are you're going to stop doubting yourself in this area. What does that look like for you?

So, you must have a vision. And if you're going to make a vision board, which I encourage everyone to do so, it'd behoove you to put it in a place where you're going to walk past it and see it every day. What wall do you face when you're lying in bed, and you first get up, and that's the first wall that you see? Put it there. It doesn't have to be huge. It can be something small for right now but create a vision board. Don't do it online, because it's not going to have the same effect on you. So, create a vision.

And the other one would be recognition. So, recognize self. Recognize what you've done. And I've talked about quick wins in the past. What have you done, say, in the last week or two weeks, that you can recognize as a quick win, perhaps? And the quicker wins that we have and that we acknowledge, the better off we're going to be, the better off our attitude's going to be. And on the rare occasion that you happen to have a bad moment during a day ... not a bad day, but a bad moment during the day, you won't be forced to think about that moment, but you'll only think about your quick win.

So, again my name's Dom Faussette, executive coach, and leadership speaker, and that three-step process is, simply put ... It was being authentic, right? And then having a vision, and then recognizing yourself. So, authenticity, have a vision, and quick wins or self-recognition. Have a wonderful day. I'll talk to you soon.

"How to Be Intentional"

What is being intentional, or intentionality?

Being intentional is nothing more than having your thoughts, your desires, your hopes, your expectations, your actions, all being aligned with where you want to go in life, and what it is you want to accomplish in life.

Some of us are very impatient with beginning our trek on our journey to success, and even though we know in the back of our mind that success does not happen overnight, we end up losing hope.

The reason why we lose hope is, well it's two reasons ... One, we're not intentional in our daily practices or daily habits. You can't expect to have daily or weekly wins if every single thing that you're doing in your life is not correlated with where you want to go.

For example, as many of you know, I've recently learned that I wasn't as intentional as I thought I was being. Yes, I was going to the gym. Yes, I was going to work. Yes, I was working on my business. Yes, I was reading books. Yes, I was not watching television. I had to re-engage some of the books I was reading on a deeper level, which for me meant, audio books, and reading the book.... the same book that I was reading at night. I'd have the audio book in the car on the way to work in the morning.

I needed to change the gym I was going to because my current gym was making me soft. I started going to a gym, where everybody was focused on building their body to compete. I'm not a competition bodybuilder. I just needed to be around tougher individuals with that mindset.

Then, I took it to the next level and started going to a Muay Thai Kickboxing gym. I don't ever plan on professionally fighting, so for me; it really tweaked the areas in my mind, to bridge the gap between my heart and my mind, even closer than what they were before.

When your body is required to be specific in its actions i.e. boxing, then it's natural for your mind to be specific in its actions. Where your passion goes, your success is typically going to flow. As I'm speaking, I'm more intentional about the topics that are being spoken about. When you are intentional, your wins happen more often. And they happen by way of other people pouring into the business, or the product that you have, or the desires that you have. And your results match what it is that you're doing and, as crazy as this sounds, when you go to sleep, your dreams match your future expectations.

Ever since I started reading more intentionally, and being more intentional with my interactions with those around me, things began to change around me. For example: Not being a jerk, being more loving, and being more open, and being more authentic with whom I was as an individual, my dreams began to change.

I do get ideas from my dreams as I believe many of you do as well. The dreams are going to come, but are you able to recognize the dreams that you're having and the one's your mind is being flooded with, to get you to next level, or stage in your life?

Again, my name is Dom Faussette, executive coach and leadership speaker. I will talk to you guys soon. Have a good day.

"How to Control Your NOW."

Many of you right now are working and focusing on who you're going to be, and there's nothing wrong with looking towards the future. But, what we fail to realize is that who you are right now is good enough to start.

You don't have to wait until you attain something or until you become someone to start working on being successful. You don't have to wait to become a leader or to start working on being a leader. You don't have to wait until you get into a relationship to start working on being a better communicator. So many times, we focus on who we're going to be, and we lose sight of who we are.

Who you are right now is enough to be great.

You don't have to wait to be something else to be great because we end up losing ourselves. We end up losing who we are. We almost end up forgetting who we are. The person you are today is just a person that you are today. And you've worked all your life to become the person that you are today.

Have you had some downs? Of course you have.

But you've also had some ups. I'm willing to bet that you've had some pretty great ups. But for some reason, we lose sight on those successes that we've had in our lives.

If you start working on who you are now, this minute, this second, today ... Don't worry about your five-year plan. Yes, it's there. It's good to take a look at it periodically. But you woke up today. What are you doing today that's going to help you to be successful, to be greater than you were yesterday? Tomorrow, you should be able to look back on today and say, "You know what? I accomplished something."

Whether it was reading a chapter in a book, and that book is in direct correlation with where you want to go, whether it's calling somebody that you haven't spoken with in a while.

You know, a lot of people continuously say to themselves, "I'm going to go to the gym, I'm going to go to the gym, I'm going to go to the gym"... Guess what? They never go.

Just go to the gym! Or if you don't have a gym membership, just go for a walk. Go for a mile walk, run a quarter of that mile, or jog. Do something that's going to push you towards being the better person that you are.

I want you to write down what you've done today. Write down what you've done today. What have you accomplished or what are you going to accomplish today that's going to get you closer to your goal? Again, we all have dreams and goals. That goes without saying. But stop putting your dreams and your goals so far out of reach that you end up not doing anything to attain them.

See, your three- to five-year plan, your three to five years is going to happen whether you want it to or not. Now, whether you're successful in that three to five years is completely up to you. But wouldn't you rather have daily successes, and every day you have a success that pushes you towards that three to five years, than hoping that you are successful in three to five years? I'm pretty certain you would.

So, if you're that person who wants to be successful, then all you need to do is START! Let's think about all the successes you've had in your life. You graduated from high school. You're in college, or you've graduated from college. You have a good job. Some of you are in good relationships. If you're not in a good relationship, just start communicating. It's really that easy.

See, stop focusing on who you want to be, because that person that you want to be, trust me when I say, it's not you. The person that you want to be is a culmination of other people that you've seen in your life. The person that I wanted to be three years ago is not the person that I am today because I started adding value to who I was as a person. Start adding value to your moment and stop worrying about adding value to your future.

If you find this blog to impact you, why don't you share it with your friends and family? Because I'm certain everybody needs just a little reminder that adding value to who you are today serves you a much greater purpose than adding value to who you want to be in the future.

"How to Increase Leadership Character."

What does your character communicate? Some of our characters need a little bit of CPR. Everybody's character needs CPR.

CPR stands for Consistency, Potential, and Respect.

Consistency: Do your followers know what they can count on you for?

I've talked in the past about leadership and leadership being influenced, nothing more, nothing less, but that being said, everybody follows.

So, for the people that are following you; are you maintaining a level of consistency in their life? In their expectations for you? And this could be at home with your kids and your spouse. This could be in the office with your team, your boss, maybe those that report to you.

Let's talk about potential.

You will never go any further than the level of your character. Let's just use zero to ten for example. If your character lid is an eight of ten, the highest your character lid will be able to go is a seven. But, if your character lid is a two, the highest you'll go is a one. So, what is it that you can do? This is a question that you have to ask yourself. What is it that you can do to increase that character lid from a leadership standpoint in your life, right? To increase your ability to increase potential in your life.

Let's talk about respect.

There are so many variations of what respect means to different people. And it's really about putting people before yourself, right? Especially if you're in a team environment, which at home, at work, or on a sports team, respect is huge, I mean, it's, you know what it is? It's servant leadership. And servant leadership, as I talked about in the past, is about digging in, putting yourself last and getting out of your team what they want from you. And let me explain that.

Your team wants consistency. Your team wants you to operate at the highest capacity at all times. When you do that, you get respect. In the event you can't, and you tell them why you can't, you get respect. If you've made a mistake and you own up to it, you get respect. Nobody's expecting anybody to walk on water. Nobody's expecting anybody to be perfect all the time. And if you feel that they are, then you need to ask why or get clarity on one's expectations for you.

So again, we're talking about character and the building of one's character. I said in the past, when you're talking to people, you need to be a person of your word. A lot of times people will, I don't know, feel guilty and make promises or over-promise because they feel that's what the person wants to hear. Why don't you tell the person what it is you want to say and what it is that you feel?

And this really works in an office environment. Don't take on every single task, because what that's going to do, it's going to decrease your character, it's going to hurt it, it's going to hurt your potential that's perceived by people around you.

So, again, your character needs CPR. That's Consistency, Potential, and Respect. Those three areas, if you were to increase your level of consistency, your level of potential and the level of respect that others have for you, your ability to lead is going to drastically increase. Your ability to be successful in self and feel self-valued is going to drastically increase.

I want you to focus on these areas.

"This Statement Will Stop Your Growth."

Last night I had the fortunate pleasure of a forty-five-minute consultation with an individual with an extremely high IQ. The forty-five-minute consultation turned into a two-hour consultation, as many of my consultations do.

I find it odd that most my clients have a very high IQ, but one thing I don't find odd is what happens in their thirties and forties. They are praised all throughout high school, and they are the man or woman of the hour all throughout college. They do pretty well into the early stages of their career.

The problem after that is there is no process or syllabus in place to kind of get to that next stage in life.

He and I spoke, like I said, for two hours. He's an engineer, one of the brightest young men I've probably ever met outside of the military realm. I've known of him and he's known me for about seven or eight years. He's seen me progress. He reached out to me back in July or August. I sent him my three-part questionnaire, and I hadn't heard back from him. Then recently, he sent me the completed questionnaire.

A couple of the statements that he made, I hear a lot from people, especially intelligent people ... one thing that caught me off guard or that struck me odd was the fact that he said, "I don't care what people think."

Let me explain: individuals that think that way or make that statement... you can't successfully maneuver or progress in your career and not care what people think. Not only can you not care what people think, but you must kind of know what they're thinking before they think it, and you should have the ability to make them think what you want them to think about you to overcome any negative perceptions they have about you.

If you're accustomed to doing something one way, but the person that say, signs your paychecks or the gatekeeper to your promotion is the one that has these misconceptions or misperceptions about you, then you need to care what they think about you. Your focus needs to be how to negate any negative thoughts that come your way and how to change their thought process about you.

At the end of the day, it's about earning the income that you're worth. This individual is well underpaid for the job that he does. One of the other statements he made was, "It's common in this industry."

I said, "Bro, you are too educated, and you've been a part of too many think tanks, too many initiatives to be paid what you're paid."

After two hours, we had some insight, but I bring this up to say that you're not the only one that is underpaid. You're not the only one that may come off like a jerk at times. You're not the only one that can be successful and maybe think it's owed to them to be successful.

Let me explain it to you. There's a game that's got to get played for you to progress in your career, and that is caring about what people think about you. You have to understand what people think about you. When you know what somebody thinks about you, it makes it very easy for you to play to their next move.

The only way to win at it is to think way outside of the box and do things differently than the way you are currently doing them. Yes, what you've done thus far has gotten you here, but how do we open that lid and get you to your next level? How do you open your lid and get you to that next level?

Life is a game. You must win at it.

How to connect with Dom Faussette

Company: Think React Lead Inc.

LinkedIn: https://www.linkedin.com/in/domfaussette

Website: www.DomFaussette.com

Instagram: @DomFaussette

FaceBook: Dom Faussette